# EUROPEAN UNION
# FACTS & FIGURES

# EUROPEAN COUNTRIES TODAY

## TITLES IN THE SERIES

# EUROPEAN UNION
# FACTS & FIGURES

Dominic J. Ainsley

**MASON CREST**

Mason Crest
450 Parkway Drive, Suite D
Broomall, Pennsylvania PA 19008
(866) MCP-BOOK (toll free)

First printing
9 8 7 6 5 4 3 2 1

ISBN: 978-1-4222-3982-7
Series ISBN: 978-1-4222-3977-3
ebook ISBN: 978-1-4222-7797-3

Printed in the United States of America

Library of Congress Cataloging-in-Publication Data

Names: Ainsley, Dominic J., author.
Title: European Union : facts & figures / Dominic J. Ainsley.
Description: Broomall, Pennsylvania : Mason Crest, an imprint of National
  Highlights, Inc., [2018] | Series: European countries today | Includes index.
Identifiers: LCCN 2018007573 (print) | LCCN 2018018829 (ebook) | ISBN
  9781422277973 (eBook) | ISBN 9781422239827 (Hardback) | ISBN 9781422239773 (Series)
Subjects: LCSH: European Union--History. | European Union countries--Politics
  and government. | European Union countries--Economic integration.
Classification: LCC JN30 (ebook) | LCC JN30 .A383 2018 (print) | DDC
  341.242/2--dc23
LC record available at https://lccn.loc.gov/2018007573

Cover images
Above left: *Migrants arriving at a European border.*
Center left: *Euro currency.*
Below left: *British people campaigning against Brexit.*
Right: *The European Parliament Building, Brussels.*

## QR CODES AND LINKS TO THIRD-PARTY CONTENT

# CONTENTS

## KEY ICONS TO LOOK FOR:

**Words to Understand:** These words with their easy-to-understand definitions will increase the reader's understanding of the text while building vocabulary skills.

**Sidebars:** This boxed material within the main text allows readers to build knowledge, gain insights, explore possibilities, and broaden their perspectives by weaving together additional information to provide realistic and holistic perspectives.

**Educational Videos:** Readers can view videos by scanning our QR codes, providing them with additional content to supplement the text. Examples include news coverage, moments in history, speeches, iconic sports moments, and much more!

**Text-Dependent Questions:** These questions send the reader back to the text for more careful attention to the evidence presented there.

**Research Projects:** Readers are pointed toward areas of further inquiry connected to each chapter. Suggestions are provided for projects that encourage deeper research and analysis.

## Quick Facts: The European Union

**Number of Member Countries:** 28
**Official Languages:** 24 (Bulgarian, Croatian, Czech, Danish, Dutch, English, Estonian, Finnish, French, German, Greek, Hungarian, Irish, Italian, Latvian, Lithuanian, Maltese, Polish, Portuguese, Romanian, Slovak, Slovene, Spanish, Swedish)
**Motto:** *In Varietate Concordia* (United in Diversity)
**European Council's President:** Donald Tusk (Poland)
**European Commission's President:** Jean-Claude Juncker  (Luxembourg)
**European Parliament's President:** Martin Schulz (Germany)
**Total Area:** 2,783,723 square miles (4,479,968 sq. km)
**Population:** 516,195,432
**GDP:** $16.52 trillion
**Per Capita GDP:** $39,200
**Formation:**
> Declared: February 7, 1992, with the signing of the Maastricht Treaty
> Recognized: November 1, 1993, with the ratification of the Maastricht Treaty

**Community Currency:** euro. Currently 19 of the 28 member states have adopted the euro as their currency
**Anthem:** "Ode to Joy"
**Flag:** Blue background with 12 gold stars arranged in a circle
> **Official Day:** Europe Day, May 9

Source: www.cia.gov 2017

RUSSIA

AINE

TURKE

CYPRUS

## The European Flag

The history of the flag dates back to 1955 when the Council of Europe, which defends human rights and promotes European culture, chose the present design for its own use. In the years that followed, it encouraged the emerging European institutions to adopt the same flag.

In 1985, the flag was adopted by the European Community and was then inherited by the European Union (EU) in 1993. The European flag symbolizes both the European Union and, more broadly, the identity and unity of Europe.

It features a circle of twelve gold stars on a blue background, which stand for the ideals of unity, solidarity, and harmony among the peoples of Europe. The twelve stars also represent completeness and perfection.

**ABOVE:** *The flags of European Union members fly outside the European Parliament Building in Strasbourg.*

***ABOVE:*** *Exterior of the European Parliament Building in Brussels, Belgium. The legislative arm of the EU is located at this site.*

***ABOVE:*** *After World War II, the citizens of Europe had had enough of conflict and were looking toward a more secure future.*

# Chapter One
# THE HISTORIC PATH TO THE EUROPEAN UNION

By the beginning of the twentieth century, the people of Europe had grown tired of the constant wars between its various countries. Hopes rose for a union that would allow the citizens of Europe to trade with one another, travel, and support each other's interests. These hopes were postponed by two great wars during the first half of the twentieth century–World War I (1914–18) and World War II (1939–45). However, by the mid-twentieth century, those people had resisted the forces of hatred and **dictatorship** during these wars, and then worked even harder to create a union of European nations that could live in peaceful cooperation. World leaders who supported the new European order included Konrad Adenauer of Germany, Winston Churchill of Britain, and Robert Schuman of France.

**ABOVE:** *Sir Winston Churchill's victory salute in May 1943.*

During this period, Schuman, who was France's foreign affairs minister, put into practice an idea orignally proposed by Jean Monnet: to set up a European Coal and Steel Community, known as the ECSC. The ECSC was officially created by the Treaty of Paris in 1951, and established a common market in coal and steel. Having a common market meant that steps had been taken to allow various countries within Europe to do business with one another more easily.

Sharing the new common market healed some of the hard feelings between the countries that had just been at war with each other, and led industry toward peaceful uses of materials that had previously been used for war.

The ECSC was the first step in the process that led to the EU as we now know it. In fact, the ECSC's goal has been largely achieved today—goods move freely across borders, with little paperwork and few if any customs duties (the fees that are paid when goods travel between countries).

In 1957, the Treaty of Rome set up the European Economic Community, the EEC. The goals of the EEC went further than ECSC's goals for free trade. These new, more ambitious goals included social progress, economic

***ABOVE:*** *On March 19, 1958, the first meeting of the European Parliamentary Assembly was held in Strasbourg under the presidency of Robert Schuman.*

***ABOVE:*** *The Palazzo dei Conservatori, where the Treaty of Rome was signed in 1957.*

improvement, and the continual improvement of social and living conditions. The EEC originally had six member countries: Belgium, France, Germany, Italy, Luxembourg, and the Netherlands. Over the years, the EEC evolved into today's EU.

The EU has always been open to states that are able to meet its economic requirements and implement its rules. For example, EU member states must agree to abide by a **customs union**, a single market, and an economic and **monetary union**.

Common policies for all member states (mostly for trade and agriculture), were first set up in the 1960s, and customs duties were removed on July 1, 1968. All of these economic and social policies worked so well that Denmark, Ireland, and the United Kingdom decided to join the EU in 1973, bringing the total number of member states to nine. At that time, the EU also began to take on even more tasks, including new social, regional, and environmental policies. To put these policies into practice, the European Regional Development Fund was set up in 1975.

Also, in the early 1970s the EU realized it needed a monetary union. At the same time though, the United States decided to suspend the dollar's convertability to gold. This decision gave rise to a period of great

**ABOVE:** *Konrad Adenauer served as the first postwar Chancellor of the Federal Republic of Germany from 1949 to 1963.*

**ABOVE:** *Jacques Delors was the eighth president of the European Commission.*

***ABOVE:*** *The Old Royal Palace is the first royal palace of modern Greece, completed in 1843. It has housed the Hellenic Parliament in Athens since 1934. The directorate of European Affairs also has an office at this site.*

instability in the world's money markets, which was then worsened by the oil crises of 1973 and 1979.

Finally, the European Monetary System (EMS) began in 1979 and helped stabilize currency exchange rates between European countries and the rest of the world. The EMS encouraged EU member states to pass their own strict policies within their own countries while also sharing power with each other.

In 1981, Greece joined the EU, followed by Spain and Portugal in 1986. These new entries made it urgent to introduce structural programs, such as the first Integrated Mediterranean Programmes, which was aimed at reducing the economic gap between the richest and the poorest member states.

During the 1970s and 1980s, the EU began to play a more prominent role outside of Europe. For instance, between 1975 and 1989, the EU signed a

**ABOVE:** *Government buildings where the Maastricht Treaty was signed on February 7, 1992, in Maastricht, the Netherlands.*

series of conventions with African countries and island nations of the Caribbean and the Pacific. Known as Lomé I, II, III, and IV, the conventions focused on aid and trade policies. These conventions eventually led to the Cotonou Agreement of June 2000, which had the goal of creating a common foreign and security policy for these countries.

The worldwide recession during the early 1980s caused great concern in Europe, but in 1985 Jacques Delors, president of the Economic Commission of

**ABOVE:** *A monument to the Maastricht Treaty outside the Limburg Province government buildings, Maastricht.*

the European Union, published a white paper setting a timetable for completing the European single market by January 1, 1993. The European single market would break down many of the divisions between the countries' economies, allowing them to trade as if they were all part of one large economic system. The policies suggested within the Delors white paper became known as the Single European Act, and it was signed in February 1986. The act became official on July 1, 1987.

In Maastricht, in the Netherlands, on December 1991, the Treaty on European Union was passed and became officially recognized on November 1, 1993. Within this treaty, EU institutions were given greater responsibilities, and what we would now recognize as the EU was created. At that point, the EEC was renamed the European Community. Original goals included the creation of a monetary union by 1999, European citizenship, and new common policies, including a European foreign and security policy. When Austria, Finland, and Sweden joined on January 1, 1995, there were now fifteen members. Twelve of these countries replaced their currencies with the euro on January 1, 2002, a currency which soon took on a similar status to the US dollar.

In Lisbon, March 2000, a meeting took place to discuss strategies for modernizing Europe's economy so that the countries of Europe could better compete in the world market. The Lisbon Strategy, which arose from this meeting, opened up all sectors to competition, encouraged innovation and business investment, and aimed to modernize Europe's education systems to meet the needs of an information society.

## Important Treaties of the European Union

Treaty of Paris (1951)
Treaty of Rome (1957)
Merger Treaty (1965)
Schengen Agreement (1985)
Single European Act (1986)

Maastricht Treaty (1992)
Amsterdam Treaty (1997)
Treaty of Nice (2001)
Treaty of Lisbon (2007)

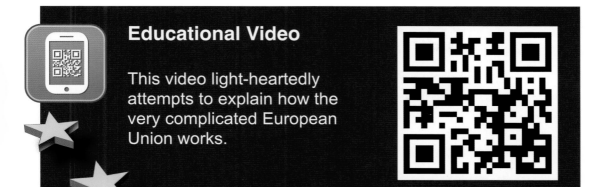

## Educational Video

This video light-heartedly attempts to explain how the very complicated European Union works.

***ABOVE:*** *Not all EU members have joined the euro single currency. Sweden for example, has chosen to keep the krona.*

## Member Countries

| | | |
|---|---|---|
| Austria | Greece | Romania |
| Belgium | Hungary | Slovakia |
| Bulgaria | Ireland | Slovenia |
| Croatia | Italy | Spain |
| Cyprus | Latvia | Sweden |
| Czech Republic | Lithuania | United Kingdom |
| Denmark | Luxembourg | *(Brexit: For the time* |
| Estonia | Malta | *being, the United* |
| Finland | Netherlands | *Kingdom remains a full* |
| France | Poland | *member of the EU.)* |
| Germany | Portugal | |

Almost as soon as the EU grew to fifteen members, another twelve asked to be admitted. In the mid 1990s, applications came from former Eastern Bloc Bulgaria, Czech Republic, Hungary, Poland, Romania, and Slovakia.

After the fall of communism in 1990, the EU supported democratization in former communist countries, giving them technical and financial assistance as they introduced market economies. Following this aid, three Baltic states that had been part of the Soviet Union (Estonia, Latvia, Lithuania), one republic of the former Yugoslavia (Slovenia), and two Mediterranean countries (Cyprus and Malta) requested admittance to the EU.

For ten of these twelve candidate countries, the negotiations were completed on December 13, 2002, in Copenhagen. By 2004, the EU had increased its membership five times, and had expanded to twenty-five member states. The enlargement in 2004 brought in eight countries from Central and Eastern Europe, and the Mediterranean islands of Malta and Cyprus. With the 450 million people of its twenty-five member states, the EU had more citizens than the combined populations of the United States and Russia. However, the ten new countries were poorer than the EU average, so raising their standard of

***ABOVE:*** *The 28 member states of the EU represented by their individual flags.*

**ABOVE:** *Zagreb, the capital of Croatia. The people of Croatia were proud and excited to join the European Union in 2013.*

living has been a priority of all the member states. The most recent countries to join the EU were Romania and Bulgaria in 2007 and Croatia in 2013, bringing the total number of member states to twenty-eight.

There are five new candidate countries hoping to join the EU: Albania, Montenegro, Serbia, Turkey, and the former Yugoslav Republic of Macedonia. Potential candidates for the future are Bosnia and Herzegovina, and Kosovo.

In the last fifty years, the EU has become the world's second-largest economy, with nineteen countries sharing the single currency. It is a growing political force in world events, and its size and importance will continue to grow in the twenty-first century.

***ABOVE:*** *A major demonstration in London against the UK leaving the EU. "Brexit" has caused deep divisions in the UK, with many worried it will harm the economy.*

In recent years, some EU countries have begun to lose their trust in the EU and its institutions. This has been linked to a rise in populist right-wing parties who are opposed to EU policies. Countries who view the EU least favorably are the UK, France, and Spain, to name a few. In 2016, a referendum was held in the UK asking British citizens if the country should remain a member of the EU. The referendum resulted in the majority of its citizens voting in favor to leave the EU. The popular term for the UK's prospective withdrawal from the EU is Brexit, and is a process that could take years.

**ABOVE:** *The prime minister of the UK, Theresa May, with the French president, Emmanuel Macron, in a press conference at the Élysée Palace, following talks on cyber and national security in 2017.*

**ABOVE:** *The UK is currently in talks to leave the EU. However, its withdrawal is proving difficult to negotiate and potentially very expensive for UK taxpayers.*

## Text-Dependent Questions

1. Whose original idea was it to set up a European Coal and Steel Community?

2. What were the goals of the Treaty of Rome?

3. Name the six original member countries of the EEC.

## Research Project

Write a report describing how the EU has changed since its creation.

## Words to Understand

**cooperation:** Association of persons for common benefit.

**federation:** The act of joining together separate organizations or states.

**parliament:** An assembly that is the highest legislative body of a country.

**ABOVE:** *The city of Strasbourg in France is the official seat of the European Parliament. The institution is legally bound to meet there twelve sessions a year, lasting about four days each. Other work takes place in Brussels and Luxembourg City.*

# Chapter Two
# HOW THE EUROPEAN UNION WORKS

Unlike the United States, the EU is not a **federation**. And unlike the United Nations (UN), it is not simply a forum to promote cooperation between governments. Instead, member states of the EU keep their own governments, but at the same time they allow European institutions to make some of their decisions.

The three decision-making bodies that create the laws within the entire EU are the European Parliament (which is elected democratically by European citizens), the Council of the European Union (whose members represent individual member states), and the European Commission (which represents the entire EU). Rules for these institutions are written into treaties, which are agreed on by the various branches of government within each of the member states.

Treaties are amended each time new member states join, which is usually every decade or so. Treaties have allowed the EU to gradually formulate more and more social, environmental, and regional policies. For example, the Treaty of Maastricht introduced two new areas of **cooperation** between member states: defense and justice. .

Other important treaties include the Single European Act (SEA), which was ratified in February 1986 and established by July 1987. This act prepared the countries of the EU for trading with each other within a single market economy. The Treaty of Amsterdam was signed on October 2, 1997, and became effective on May 1, 1999. This treaty amended other European and EU Community treaties. The Treaty of Nice was signed on February 26, 2001, and was implemented on February 1, 2003. This treaty amended the other treaties in order to allow other countries to join the EU more easily. Finally, the Treaty of

***ABOVE:*** *The European Central Bank in Frankfurt, Germany, is the central bank for the euro and administers the monetary policy of the eurozone.*

**ABOVE:** *Donald Tusk has been president of the European Council since 2014. Previously he was prime minister of Poland (2007–14).*

Lisbon was signed on December 13, 2007, and implemented on December 1, 2009. This treaty made the EU more democratic and efficient, and better able to address important global problems, such as climate change.

Treaties also establish the rules for European decision-making. There are three main methods for enacting laws: (1) in police and judicial matters, to revise treaties, and to alter economic policy, **parliament** must provide its opinion or consultation; (2) in jobs for the European Central Bank (ECB), certain international agreements, and to accept new member states, the European Council has to attain parliament's assent; and (3) in regard to the environment, education, and employment, parliament shares power with the Council of the European Union by codecision.

***ABOVE:*** *Jean-Claude Juncker has been president of the European Commission since 2014. Prior to this he was prime minister of Luxembourg (1995–2013).*

The European Parliament shares with the European Council the power to make laws. It also supervises the EU institutions; in particular, the European Commission. It can reject nominations of the Commission, and has the right to censure the Commission as a whole. It shares with the Council authority over the budget.

The Council of the European Union is the legislative arm of the union. The position of President of the European Council became a permanent and full-time role in 2009, following the Treaty of Lisbon. The president is elected for a two-and-a-half-year term. The current president is Donald Tusk. The European Council meets approximately four times a year, although the president can convene additional meetings in emergencies. As to which members attend a particular meeting depends on the issues under discussion.

**ABOVE:** *Inside the interior of the European Parliament in Brussels.*

## Committees that make up the council include:

- General Affairs and Financial Affairs
- Economic and Financial Affairs
- Employment
- Social Policy
- Health and Consumer Affairs
- Competitiveness
- Transport, Telecommunications, and Energy
- Agriculture and Fisheries
- Environment
- Education
- Youth and Culture

**ABOVE:** *Wind turbines. The EU has set goals for cutting greenhouse gas emissions and encourages member countries to adopt renewable power sources.*

**ABOVE:** *The EU has rules for responsible fishing and sets quotas (the amount of fish each member country can catch).*

## Where is the EU Located?

The seven institutions of the European Union are:

1. **European Parliament**
2. **European Council**
3. **Council of the European Union**
4. **European Commission**
5. **Court of Justice of the European Union**
6. **European Central Bank**
7. **Court of Auditors**

These institutions are located in Brussels, Strasbourg, Luxembourg, and Frankfurt. EU agencies and other bodies are located across the EU. Over the years, however, Brussels has become the principal seat of the EU.

## The Council has six main responsibilities:

- It passes laws, often jointly, with the European Parliament.
- It coordinates the broad economic policies of EU members.
- It concludes international agreements between the EU and one or more states.
- It approves the budget of the European Parliament.
- It develops the EU's common foreign and security policy.
- It mediates between national courts and police in criminal matters.

In January 2003, for example, the European Union Police Mission began operations in Bosnia and Herzegovina, taking over the civilian aspects of crisis management from UN peacekeepers. To enable the EU to respond more effectively to international crises, the European Council decided at the Helsinki

**ABOVE:** *The Berlaymont building in Brussels is the headquarters of the European Commission.*

Summit meeting in December 1999 that the Union would create a Rapid Rotation Force of up to 60,000 military personnel that could be deployed within sixty days and be kept in operation for at least a year.

An example of the work of the Committee on Justice and Home Affairs, one of the council's individual committees, is its work on the problems of drugs, terrorism, international fraud, trafficking in human beings, and the sexual exploitation of children. Such work is accomplished because of cooperation between EU member states.

**ABOVE:** *The Europa building, seat of the European Council, was built on the former site of the Residence Palace in Brussels. It combines the art deco style of the original building with a postmodern design.*

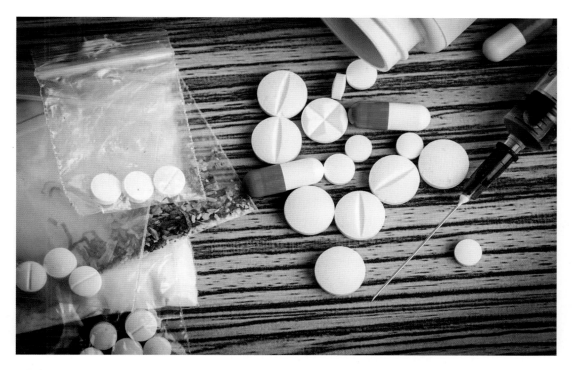

***ABOVE:*** *The Committee on Justice and Home Affairs works tirelessly to eradicate the complex problems associated with drug misuse.*

In Brussels, each member state has a permanent representative, called an ambassador, to the European Council. Ambassadors meet weekly to prepare the work of the Council.

The Council's president is aided by the General Secretariat. Decisions in the Council are decided by vote. On November 1, 2014, a new system replaced the old one. In accordance with the new procedure, when the Council votes on a proposal, a qualified majority is reached if two conditions are met:

1. 55 percent of member states vote in favor (in practice this means 16 out of 28).
2. The proposal is supported by member states representing 65 percent of the total EU population.

This new procedure is known as the "double majority" rule.

The European Commission suggests legislation and implements decisions made by the Parliament and the Council. Together, the governments within the EU agree on a president. The president and the representatives of members choose twenty-eight other members of the European Commission. The Parliament then interviews and approves the nominees. Each nominee appears before the European Parliament to explain their vision and answer questions. Parliament then votes on whether to accept the nominees as a team. Finally, they are appointed by the European Council by a qualified majority. The current Commission's term of office runs until October 31, 2019.

There are 24,000 officials, experts, and translators who do the work of the European Commission at its seat, which is in Brussels, Belgium. The Commission's main duties include proposing legislation to Parliament and the Council, managing and implementing EU policies and its budget, enforcing European Law with the Court of Justice, and representing the EU on the world stage. The European Commission proposes action only if it believes national, regional, or local interests can't solve a problem. This is called the "subsidiary principle."

The Court of Justice makes legal judgments on cases brought before it. There is one judge from each EU member state, with eleven advocates general. The advocates assist judges and present reasoned opinions. Members of both courts are appointed for renewable terms of six years.

Common cases heard by the courts include requests for a preliminary ruling. This helps various EU member states to interpret laws the same way. There are also "proceedings for failure to fulfill an obligation," when any member of the EU fails to keep a promise. And there are also proceedings for "annulment," when a claim is made that a law is illegal, as well as "failures to act," when European Parliament or the European Commission fail to take a required action.

The European Court of Auditors is independent of other institutions and checks that EU funds are used properly. There is one auditor from each country handling EU income or expenditure. The ECB was set up in 1998. It manages the euro within the nineteen countries that have now adopted it as their currency. Its main job is keeping inflation under control.

**ABOVE:** *Antonio Tajani is an Italian politician who has served as president of the European Parliament since January 2017.*

***ABOVE:*** *The two towers of the European Court of Justice in Kirchberg, Luxembourg.*

Apart from institutions, there are also more than thirty agencies within the EU. Agencies differ from institutions in that they are not provided for by treaties, but rather, have been created by individual pieces of legislation and are set up to perform specific tasks.

The European Economic and Social Committee represents civil society—such as trade unions, farmers, and consumers. The Committee of the Regions represents regional and local authorities with respect to issues like the environment, education, or transportation. The European Investment Bank finances EU projects. Last of all, the European Ombudsman uncovers maladministration of the EU. It is an intermediary between citizens and the EU, which looks at complaints from citizens of the member states.

## Text-Dependent Questions

1. Name three EU treaties.

2. Who is the current president of the European Council?

3. What does the European Court of Auditors do?

## Research Project

Imagine you represent a country asking for admission to the EU. Write a report on why admission is important for your country.

## Words to Understand

**free market:** An economy operating by free competition.

**legislation:** The process of making laws.

**single market:** A group of countries that have an agreement which allows goods to be moved, bought, or sold between them very easily.

***ABOVE:*** *The euro (sign: €; code: EUR) is the official currency of the eurozone. At present, nineteen of the twenty-eight member states of the European Union use the euro. It came into official circulation on January 1, 2002. Non-EU countries including Kosovo, Montenegro, and some microstates also use the euro.*

# Chapter Three
# THE EUROPEAN UNION & EUROPE'S ECONOMY

The makeup of the European economy has changed greatly during the past six decades. In 1958, 23 percent of the population in the six countries of the EEC relied on farming for a job. By 2014, less than 5 percent of the twenty-eight members of the EU relied on farming. There has been a similar drop in the percentage working in industry: In 1958 it was 40 percent but in 2014 it was only 21 percent. Today, service industries are the largest source of jobs, with 73 percent of the EU's population working in this sector in 2014 compared to 37 percent in 1958.

**Three key steps to breaking down barriers to trade within the EU have been**

- the creation of a customs union (which began the process of free trade),
- the establishment of a **single market** (which eliminated much of the paperwork involved with trade),
- the economic and monetary union (which removed barriers to cross-border investment).

**Educational Video**

EU trade policy explained. EU trade policy sets the direction for trade and investment in and out of the EU.

## The National Holiday

Europe Day celebrates peace and unity in Europe and is held every year on May 9. The date marks the day in 1950 when Robert Schuman proposed the creation of what became the European Coal and Steel Community. Schuman's original vision was to create an institution to manage coal and steel production, but his proposal is considered to be the beginning of what is now the European Union.

Each year in early May, EU institutions are open to the public in Brussels and Strasbourg. Regional and local EU offices in Europe and other countries organize events and activities for visitors to enjoy. At this time, there is an opportunity for thousands of people to take part in visits, debates, concerts, and other events to mark the day, and to celebrate and raise awareness about the EU and the achievements it has made.

When the customs union was completed in 1968, free trade quickly opened up in the EU. Businesses from Lapland to Sicily, and from Portugal's Atlantic islands to the EU's easternmost borders, no longer paid customs duties. The customs union also standardized duties on imports that arrived from various parts of the world. As a result, EU importers have begun to bring shipments in bulk that they then break down for delivery to various member states.

Because of the customs union, by 1970, member states were trading six times as much between themselves as they had twelve years earlier. They were also trading three times as much with the rest of the world. Their economies doubled in size and expanded faster than the US economy. After the successes of the customs union, some obstacles still remained, particularly in developing common EU standards for issues such as environmental regulation and technical requirements. The SEA, with its plans for the European single market, was signed in 1986, and set 1992 as a target for eliminating many of the remaining trade barriers in the EU. Putting the single market in place took more than a thousand pieces of **legislation** over seven years. It eased checks on goods as they crossed borders, and it allowed countries to trust one another's standards and technologies. Competition was then introduced into areas traditionally held by monopolies, such as telecommunications, airlines, the railways, postal services, gas, and electricity.

***ABOVE:*** *The creation of a customs union meant goods could be traded freely within the EU without tariffs, lengthy paperwork, or border controls.*

## The Euro

The euro is the most tangible proof of European integration: it is the common currency in nineteen out of twenty-eight EU countries and used by some 338.6 million people every day. The benefits of the common currency are immediately obvious to anyone traveling abroad or shopping online on websites based in another eurozone country.

Source: europa.eu 2017

**Between 1992 and today, the EU's single market has**

• been a key factor in boosting investment within the EU;
• made the EU internationally competitive;
• allocated skills, by giving workers the choice to work with various countries;
• boosted purchasing power by putting pressure on prices;
• generated billions of euros in prosperity;
• contributed to an increase in manufactured goods.

Part of the advantage of the single market economy has been the introduction of the euro. The standardization of the euro within the EU ensures a low inflation environment, and it gives European countries an international currency with which to deal with the rest of the world.

Euro notes and coins were introduced on January 1, 2002, in the form of seven different notes and eight different coins. Each coin has a euro design on one side and a symbol of its specific country on the other. Unlike the coins, euro notes are standard from country to country. Before these coins and notes were introduced, Europeans were burdened by the cost of changing their money as they traveled from country to country. Today, however, people can shop more efficiently, even comparing prices for goods as those prices differ from country to country.

Another hurdle to overcome within the single market was the continual enlargement of the EU. Initial costs of expansion are high as the EU helps newcomers complete the transition to becoming **free market** economies. However, all member states benefit since competition and increased personal mobility are good for growth. Also, newcomers expect 1 percent more growth each year from membership.

In 1990, the EU lifted its last remaining restrictions on taking money from one member state to another. Because of these lifted restrictions, governments were no longer able to turn to central banks to print money to bail them out if they could not balance their budgets. In 1994, the European Monetary Institute was formed, the forerunner of today's ECB. EU member states now agree on a

***ABOVE:*** *Eurozone countries are free to purchase goods and services across the EU without having to worry about currency exchange rates or import tariffs.*

system of "multilateral surveillance" to watch out for instances when one member state's decisions might have adverse effects on the economies of the others.

The Stability and Growth Pact commits all EU member states to the principle of budgets that are at least *nearly* balanced. This pact keeps governments from increasing taxes, and it also frees governments to spend money on its citizens rather than on debt repayments. If economic growth does slow within a country, some borrowing may be justified; however, the Stability and Growth Pact ensures that an excessive deficit in one EU country does not have a negative effect on the others.

The ECB plays a crucial role in achieving stability for the euro area. It does so by setting the interest rates it uses in its dealings with banks, which in turn

**ABOVE:** *The euro is as important to the world's economy as the US dollar.*

act as a baseline for all euro-area interest rates. The bank also manages the currency reserves of all of the euro area, and has the power to buy and sell foreign exchange on international currency markets.

When the euro was introduced in 1999, European governments were in most cases immediately paying less interest on money they borrowed. A low inflation environment, in a market where there were plenty of buyers and sellers, also aids the governments. Lower interest rates keep the cost of debt repayment down and leave governments more money to spend on health, pensions, social welfare, or the inner workings of their governments.

Not only do member states benefit from the EU's new economy, but many other countries throughout the world benefit as well. Many countries are now borrowing in euros because it is an internationally recognized currency. Also, the euro gives countries another option to diversify their holdings. Today, the euro is increasingly competitive with the US dollar for use by banks as reserve currency (currency kept for monetary crises).

## Text-Dependent Questions

1. What are the benefits of a single currency?

2. What is the role of the European Central Bank (ECB)?

3. Why is a low-inflation economy beneficial?

## Research Project

Make a map of Europe and color-code the members of the EU based on the year they joined.

## Words to Understand

**budget:** To plan to spend (an amount of money) for a particular purpose.

**initiative:** Energy shown in getting action started.

**social networking:** The creation and maintenance of relationships, especially online.

***ABOVE:*** *eLearning progams focus on getting the most from computer technology, for all citizens across the EU.*

# Chapter Four
# THE EUROPEAN UNION & A KNOWLEDGE-BASED SOCIETY

Article 2 of the Treaty on European Union promises "to promote economic and social progress and a high level of employment." One of the ways the EU has gone about fulfilling this promise is the eEurope **initiative**. This initiative is based on the belief that getting more European citizens online will create jobs and make European industries more competitive with the rest of the world.

The eEurope initiative was introduced by the European Commission in November 1999. In addition to economic benefits, the initiative was also

**ABOVE:** *The EU is committed to getting all households connected to the internet.*

## Knowledge-Based Society

A knowledge-based society refers a country or region that generates its success through knowledge. It can adapt to the changing economic and political dynamics of the modern world. Societies such as these are well educated, and therefore rely on the knowledge of their citizens to drive the innovation, entrepreneurship, and dynamism of that society's economy.

concerned with the benefits to education, government services, health, and cultural entertainment that would come from technology improvements. The eEurope initiative has four component programs: eLearning, eHealth, eGovernment, and eBusiness. All these progams focus on bringing computer

***ABOVE:*** *Information technology is an important part of a knowledge-based society.*

***ABOVE:*** *"The Cloud" is a type of computing that relies on shared computer resources rather than having local servers or personal devices to handle applications.*

technology to all citizens, not just a privileged few. At the EU March 2000 Summit in Lisbon, the European heads of state set a goal for the EU to be the most competitive knowledge-based society by 2010.

At the time of the Lisbon Summit, only 18 percent of European households had Internet access. By 2016, 85 percent of European households had access to the Internet at home. The EU helped achieve this improvement by developing cheaper, faster, and more secure Internet access through encouraging competition. Competitors now challenge national suppliers who once held monopolies on Internet access.

EU countries are not required to make changes to their own laws to achieve the goals, just to share information through the "open coordination method."

**EU leaders at the March 2000 Lisbon Summit agreed that in order to fulfill the 1999 eEurope initiative**

• businesses and citizens must have access to inexpensive, world-class communications;
• every citizen must be equipped with skills to live in an information society;
• a high priority must be given to lifelong learning.

By sharing information, and by spending EU **budget** money on programs to adapt new technologies in poorer regions, progress on the three agreement points has been reached. EU leaders have agreed to keep increasing spending on research so that the development of technology will continue.

Mobile internet usage in the EU has recorded notable growth. The fastest growth has been seen in Germany, Estonia, Spain, and Hungary.

Services based on cloud computing technology allow users to store large files or use software on a server run over the Internet. Cloud services are a relatively new phenomenon compared with web applications for **social networking**, listening to music, or watching films. One of the main challenges faced when measuring the usage of cloud services is being able to make a clear distinction between these and other online services. In 2014, 21 percent of the EU population aged 16 to 74 reported having used Internet storage space to save documents, pictures, music, videos, or other files.

EU leaders know that Internet access alone is not enough to achieve their goals. Thus, the eLearning program is also an

**ABOVE:** *Portuguese economist Maria João Rodrigues played an important role in the Lisbon Strategy.*

**ABOVE:** *The EU has encouraged its member states to set up online government services that can be used for a number of purposes. The above is a passport application website.*

important part of the eEurope initiative. The EU finances education programs so that its citizens acquire digital literacy and computer skills for future jobs and social interaction. The eLearning program coordinates national efforts to modernize education systems. The program aims to link all schools and training centers through the Internet.

The eLearning program also has an eContent component. The EU recognized that language barriers keep its citizens from using the Internet. In 2003, 75 percent of all websites were in English. The eContent component seeks to increase the use of other languages on the Internet and create sites for all member citizens to use.

With the expected increase in economic growth and trained technology users, the EU hopes to implement its eGovernment and eHealth programs. The eGovernment program will allow citizens to use government services such as these through easy computer access:

- income tax services
- job search services
- social security contributions
- drivers' licenses
- car registrations
- declarations of theft to the police
- birth and marriage certificates
- enrollment in universities
- passport applications

**ABOVE:** *The EU's eHealth program encourages the use of technology to aid accessibility to healthcare, particularly for the disabled.*

The eHealth program aims to use computer technology to improve the quality and accessibility of healthcare, particularly for the disabled. The eHealth program also encourages doctors to use the Internet to help all ages.

*RIGHT: The European Union places great emphasis on information technology. An educated society leads to prosperity for all its citizens.*

## Text-Dependent Questions

**1.** Why is it important for citizens to have access to the Internet?

**2.** Explain what the "cloud" is.

**3.** Why do language barriers prevent citizens from gaining knowledge on the Internet?

## Research Project

Write a report on why a knowledge-based society is so important in advanced nations.

## Words to Understand

**gross domestic product (GDP):** The total value of the goods and services produced by the people of a nation during a year, not including the value of income earned in foreign countries.

**modernize:** To make or become new and different, or suitable for the present time.

**pollution:** The action of making something impure and often unsafe or unsuitable for use.

**ABOVE:** *Even though Romania is a member of the EU, agricultural practices in some rural areas are still in need of modernization. With its EU accession in 2007, Romania has gained access to much-needed financing for agriculture.*

# Chapter Five
# WHAT DOES THE
# EUROPEAN UNION DO?

Many structural policies have been required so that all regions of Europe and all sectors of the economies of member states can benefit from the achievements the EU has made during the last sixty years. For example, many regional and social policies have been introduced to narrow the economic gap between rich and poor regions. The EU's regional policies allow its budget to be used to help its poorer members. Payments are used to **modernize** farming, help people find jobs, and convert old industries into modern, economically profitable ones.

***ABOVE:*** *The EU promotes the modernization of industries throughout its member states.*

# Demographic Ageing

According to *Europa EU*, in the next few decades, the proportion of elderly people in EU countries is set to rise fast, while the proportion of working-age people will fall significantly. Although enabling people to live longer is a major achievement, aging populations also present significant challenges to European economies and welfare systems. This demographic transition is viewed as one of the biggest challenges facing the EU.

**Age-related changes will have an impact on**
- pensions,
- long-term healthcare,
- education,
- unemployment transfers,
- various EU-level policy debates.

**The EU relies on three criteria to determine member state eligibility for this money:**

• when the **gross domestic product** of a member state is less than 75 percent of the EU average;
• when certain areas are being restructured, are declining, or are in economic crisis;
• when job training for workers is needed.

***ABOVE:*** *The European Commission has launched (or works closely with) various initiatives to support education and workplace training courses.*

## Population Distribution

Population distribution varies considerably from country to country, but tends to follow a pattern of coastal and river settlement, with urban agglomerations forming large hubs facilitating large scale housing, industry, and commerce; the area in and around the Netherlands, Belgium, and Luxembourg (known collectively as Benelux) is the most densely populated area in the EU.

***ABOVE:*** *Lignite (brown coal) is a dirty source of energy. Despite this, it is still mined in parts of Europe. This opencast mine is in Garzweiler, Germany.*

**ABOVE:** *The EU encourages its members to improve rail networks across Europe, making them more efficient and affordable.*

Specific programs to achieve these goals promote cooperation across borders and aid cities in crisis.

Structures within the EU have been expanded further to accommodate the new member states. Social progress is also supported by EU laws, which protect workers' health and ensure fair wages. In 1991, the European Council

**Educational Video**

Top six facts about the
European Social Charter.

# Health Care and Long-Term Care

According to *Europa EU*, health care and long-term care systems aim at providing timely access to good-quality medical care and enable people to live independently through provisions of social care, such as for patients with disabilities. This contributes to human well-being and economic prosperity and will be crucial for longer working lives in the context of an aging society.

Demographic aging will have a major impact on health care and long-term care spending. Given the scale of public expenditure on health care and long-term care, the topic is at the center of the policy debate on how to keep public finances sustainable in the future.

Public expenditure on health care and long-term care depends on several factors affecting the supply of and demand for care.

**Demand-side factors include**
- population size,
- age and gender distribution,
- health and disability status,
- individual and national wealth,
- rules regulating access to healthcare goods and services.

**Supply-side factors include**
- the availability and accessibility of services,
- patients' expectations,
- technological development,
- the regulatory framework.

**ABOVE:** *EU policies for heath care have greatly improved conditions in many countries whose health services were lacking.*

established the Community Charter of Basic Social Rights for Workers. These rights included free movement of citizens, fair pay, and improved working conditions.

EU policies have grown from their economic emphases to address environmental concerns, health, consumer rights, transportation, and education. Since most of these are cross-border issues, EU legislation is needed to resolve them. For example, because pollution knows no geographic bounds, the EU has adopted air **pollution** standards protecting the ozone layer by reducing emissions of chlorofluorcarbons (CFCs). The EU has also set new policies to conserve and manage natural resources alongside their goal of boosting Europe's technological capacity.

In 1958, the European Community set up the European Atomic Energy Community in order to remain world leaders in technology and to exploit nuclear power for peaceful purposes.

**ABOVE:** *Steps are being taken in an attempt to reduce pollution across the whole of the EU. However, air pollution continues to cause thousands of premature deaths every year.*

**ABOVE:** *The EU is committed to protecting the ozone layer, which blocks most solar ultraviolet radiation from entry into the lower atmosphere.*

## Text-Dependent Questions

1. Why does the EU help member states who struggle economically?

2. Why is pollution a cross-border issue?

3. Why was the European Atomic Energy Community set up?

## Research Project

Imagine that you live in a country that has joined the EU. Write a description how your country has changed since becoming a member state.

***ABOVE:*** *The European Court of Human Rights in Strasbourg is an international court established by the European Convention on Human Rights. Individuals, parties, or other states can bring about an application against any European state, that has signed up to the Convention if they believe this state has committed a human rights violation.*

## Chapter Six
# THE EUROPEAN UNION, FREEDOM, SECURITY & JUSTICE

Even though the EU tries to **guarantee** its citizens freedom from violence, crime, and terrorism, these problems remain major concerns for Europeans. Because of the single-market economy, such challenges must be met by the entire union, rather than by individual governments. And with its recent enlargement to twenty-eight member states, the EU has been pushed to confront these matters swiftly.

The original Treaty of Rome of 1957 never addressed issues like crime. Only later did the freedom of movement of EU's citizens make it clear that all Europeans must have the same access to justice. Therefore, later amendments to the Treaty of Rome have begun to address the protection of EU citizens. These amendments have included the Single European Act and the Treaties of Maastricht, Amsterdam, and Lisbon.

Specific policies have included a stronger emphasis on the EU's external borders, since checkpoints have slowly been abolished on borders between various European nations. Also, police forces and judicial authorities from all European countries have begun to work together to combat crime.

*RIGHT: The Schengen Area is an area comprising twenty-six EU states that have abolished border controls at their mutual borders.*

On October 15 and 16, 1999, the European Council called a special meeting at Tampere, Finland, to discuss issues of freedom, security, and justice in the EU. In the years following the meeting, steps were to be taken to protect Europe's citizens, with the European Commission being given the task of monitoring the implementation of these steps. Below are some of the major steps that were proposed during this meeting:

- establishment of a common EU policy of asylum and immigration
- establishment of a genuine "European area of justice"
- an EU-wide fight against crime
- stronger external action

With these goals in mind, the EU remains aware that policies for **justice** within the EU must be carefully balanced with policies for freedom. For example, in 1985, Belgium, France, Germany, Luxembourg, and the Netherlands agreed to abolish all checks on persons at the borders between their countries. This agreement, known as the **Schengen** Agreement, required EU citizens to present only an identity card or a

## Crossing Borders

The Schengen Agreement means that countries of Europe who signed up to the agreement can allow their citizens to travel freely across borders without having to present travel documents. Schengen has its advantages, as goods and citizens can move around more swiftly. A disadvantage of Schengen, however, is that people may pass from country to country with little scrutiny.

passport when traveling. Today, there are twenty-six Schengen countries—twenty-two EU members and four non-EU. Those four are Iceland and Norway (since 2001), Switzerland (since 2008), and Liechtenstein (since 2011). Only six of the twenty-eight EU member states are outside the Schengen zone—Bulgaria, Croatia, Cyprus, Ireland, Romania, and the UK.

Besides the possible spread of criminal activity, the rising number of immigrants is a problem associated with the EU's lack of internal borders. The Council's meeting at Tampere established common asylum procedures for all EU nations. Also, immigrants are to be judged by the same set of rules within all countries of the EU.

One immigration problem has been the activity of criminal gangs who run people-smuggling networks and exploit vulnerable human beings, especially

***ABOVE:*** *The aftermath of the terrorist attacks in Paris on November 13, 2015. The French antiterrorist force patrol the streets.*

**ABOVE:** *Hundreds of migrants and refugees walk from Slovenia to Germany in an attempt to escape from warzones or economic hardship. During this crisis, the German chancellor's policy of showing compassion to hundreds of thousands of these people was in sharp contrast to the outright hostility directed at them in several other European nations.*

### Educational Video

Syrian refugees: a human crisis revealed in a powerful short film from *National Geographic.*

***ABOVE:*** *Migrants from Libya arriving in Lampedusa, Italy. The migrants pay large sums of money to traffickers, who put them in illegal and dangerous boats. Many thousands have died crossing the Mediterranean this way.*

women and children. These criminals have become very sophisticated over the last twenty years and have learned to use European networks for their activities. Organized crime and terrorism have also become more brutal and clever across the globe within the last two decades; they are among the EU's growing concerns.

To combat such crime, the Schengen Information System is a complex database that has been set up to exchange information between countries. It allows law enforcement to exchange information on wanted people or property—for example, stolen vehicles or works of art, or persons for whom an arrest warrant or extradition request has been issued. Another way to catch

***ABOVE:*** *Legal economic migrants who enter the EU are very important to many countries as they provide a flexible and viable workforce.*

***ABOVE:*** *Europol headquarters at The Hague, Netherlands, is the European police department that coordinates with national police forces against organized crime.*

**ABOVE:** *The streamlining of European laws has made passing legislation much easier.*

criminals is to track the money made through criminal activity. To this end, the EU has passed laws to stop money laundering.

The greatest advance in security within the EU is Europol, a group of police and customs officers that services the entire union. Europol addresses such issues as drug trafficking, stolen vehicles, people smuggling, sexual exploitation of women and children, pornography, forgery, the selling of nuclear materials, terrorism, money laundering, and counterfeiting the euro.

Unfortunately, different judicial systems within the EU enforce laws in ways that confuse many who continually travel from one European country to another. Several EU programs have been set up to bring together law professionals from different member states. The Grotius Program helps lawyers and judges learn how legal systems in other European countries work. The

Falcone Program develops contacts between judges, prosecution services, and police forces. And Eurojust enables investigators from various countries to work together to solve crimes.

Finally, cooperation between courts in various countries can be hurt by differing definitions of criminal acts, as well as by sentencing variations. To deal effectively with these concerns, the EU has compiled a common penal policy, as well as a common legal framework for fighting terrorism.

Until 1997, immigration and judicial cooperation for law enforcement were matters that required cooperation between the various EU governments.

**ABOVE:** *The head office of Eurojust at The Hague.*

However, the Treaty of Amsterdam transferred these issues to the "community" domain. This move took place, however, over the course of a five-year transition period, during which decisions were shared between the European Commission and member states of the EU. The EU's goals, however are clear: to establish an enforceable system throughout all member nations, ensuring its citizens' safety and security.

*RIGHT: All the systems and offices explained in this chapter are designed to get the very best for EU citizens.*

## Text-Dependent Questions

1. In which year did the European Council hold a meeting on freedom, security, and justice in the EU at Tampere, Finland?

2. What is Europol?

3. What is Eurojust?

## Research Project

Write an essay on the Schengen Agreement. Explain in detail why it has been criticized in recent years.

## Words to Understand

**constitution:** The basic beliefs and laws of a nation, state, or social group.

**continent:** One of the great divisions of land on the globe—Africa, Antarctica, Asia, Australia, Europe, North America, or South America.

**individuality:** The qualities that make one person or thing different from all others.

***ABOVE:*** *Victor Hugo's prediction was that Europe would join as one. His vision was that each country would keep its identity, customs, and traditions. It took more than a hundred years for his dream to be realized.*

## Chapter Seven
# THE EUROPEAN UNION & THE FUTURE

In 1849, the writer Victor Hugo predicted that "a day will come when all the nations of this **continent**, without losing their distinct qualities of their glorious **individuality**, will fuse together and form the European Brotherhood." It took more than one hundred years for Hugo's dream to take shape, in the form of the EU. And even now, after another sixty years, new challenges and difficulties are still being presented.

The EU is currently a community of twenty-eight member states, with further enlargement predicted during the coming years. If this goal is reached, leaders must then decide whether to draw final geographical boundaries around the EU.

Even during such times of change, the half a billion people of the EU still

***ABOVE:*** *Victor Hugo, nineteenth-century French poet, playwright, novelist, essayist, visual artist, and statesman.*

agree on a "foundational agreement," an agreement that continues to emphasize the traditional European values of peace, security, democracy, and justice—with each of the EU's member states sharing some of its power to achieve these aims.

***ABOVE:*** *The ruins of the Chernobyl reactor in Ukraine. There has been an exclusion zone around it for over thirty years, following a nuclear accident, and the effect of its fallout is still evident in Europe. The EU has developed new technologies to ensure that other disasters of this magnitude can never happen in an EU country.*

Today's technological revolution presents economic benefits as well as risks, such as spilled oil tankers or Chernobyl-type nuclear accidents. National policies alone can't secure the economic growth of European countries. To hope to combat these problems, the EU must act as a single force.

The EU is also affected by developments in other parts of the world, such as the global rise of religious extremism, forced displacement in Africa and Asia, shifts in the balance of economic power between East and West, and US

## Potential Countries to Join the EU in the Future

Albania

Bosnia and Herzegovina

Kosovo

Macedonia

Montenegro

Serbia

Turkey

***ABOVE:*** *The city of Split is situated on the Dalmatian coast in Croatia. It is a UNESCO World Heritage Site. In 2013, Croatia joined the EU, the most recent country to do so.*

unilateralism. Because of these concerns, the EU must continue to be involved in the world's development, as well as that of its member states.

Europe must adjust to the growing number of challenges in today's world. Each new member state adds a new force that threatens to break apart the union. Countries often have short-term policies that threaten the long-term goals of the EU as a whole. Only a democratic political system with checks and

***ABOVE:*** *Supporters of the EU—Jean-Claude Juncker (president of the European Commission), Emmanuel Macron (president of France), and Angela Merkel (chancellor of Germany)—at a press conference in 2017.*

balances will allow so many various cultures to remain distinct while also working toward a single goal.

The **constitution** of the EU has been designed to simplify the policies within the treaties and to clearly explain the government's decision-making process. One purpose of this constitution is to explain the goals and ideals of the EU so that its citizens will be motivated to become part of its democratic process. Within the constitution, both the will of the people and the legitimacy of their national governments are supported.

It is still to early too know whether the constitution is the final project that completes the EU, or whether the political structures in Europe will evolve even further. But one thing is certain: the EU is a growing political and economic force in the twenty-first century world stage.

## Text-Dependent Questions

1. Who was Victor Hugo?

2. How many countries are candidates or potential candidates to join the EU?

3. What accident happened at Chernobyl?

## Research Project

Find out how many European countries are NOT in the EU and explain the reasons why they have not joined.

| | |
|---|---|
| **1914** | World War I begins; it ends in 1918. |
| **1939** | World War II begins; it ends in 1945. |
| **1951** | Treaty of Paris creates the European Coal and Steel Community. |
| **1957** | Treaty of Rome establishes the European Economic Community (EEC). |
| **1958** | The European Atomic Energy Community is established. |
| **1961** | The European Social Fund is established. |
| **1968** | All customs duties are removed for members of the EEC. |
| **1973** | Denmark, Ireland, and the United Kingdom join the EEC. |
| **1975** | The European Regional Development Fund is established. |
| **1979** | The European Monetary System begins. |
| **1981** | Greece joins the EEC. |
| **1986** | Portugal and Spain join the EEC. |
| **1987** | Single European Act is established. |
| **1990** | Communism falls in Europe. |
| **1991** | Community Charter of Basic Social Rights is established. |
| **1991** | The Treaty on European Union creates the European Union as known today; it is officially recognized on November 1, 1993. |
| **1994** | European Monetary Institute is established. |
| **1995** | Austria, Finland, and Sweden join the EU. |
| **1997** | Treaty of Amsterdam is signed, becomes effective May 1, 1999. |
| **1998** | European National Bank is established. |
| **1999** | eEurope initiative is established. |
| **2000** | The Lisbon Strategy is adopted. |
| **2001** | Treaty of Nice is signed; becomes effective February 1, 2003. |
| **2002** | The euro goes into circulation. |
| **2003** | European Union Police Mission begins operations in Bosnia and Herzegovina. |
| **2004** | The European Union expands to twenty-five members. |
| **2006** | Turkey's bid to join the European Union stalls. |
| **2007** | Romania and Bulgaria join the European Union. |
| **2008** | Global financial crisis. |
| **2009** | Treaty of Lisbon is ratified by all EU countries. |
| **2012** | European Union is awarded the Nobel Peace Prize. |
| **2013** | Croatia joins the European Union. |
| **2014** | European elections are held in 2014 and more Euroskeptics are elected into the European Parliament. |
| **2017** | European Union countries are the target of several terror attacks. |

## Further Reading

McDonald, Fergie. Marsden, Claire (project editors). *DK Eyewitness Travel Guide: Europe*. London: DK, 2017.

McCormick, John. *Understanding the European Union: A Concise Introduction.* London: Palgrave Macmillan, 2017.

Mason, David S. *A Concise History of Modern Europe: Liberty, Equality, Solidarity. London:* Rowman & Littlefield, 2015.

Steves, Rick. *Rick Steves Best of Europe*. Edmonds: Rick Steves' Europe, Inc., 2017.

## Internet Resources

**Lonely Planet: Europe: A Voyage Through History**
https://www.lonelyplanet.com/europe#experiences

**CNN: European Union Fast Facts**
http://edition.cnn.com/2013/06/06/world/europe/european-union-fast-facts/index.html

**Profile: European Union**
http://news.bbc.co.uk/1/hi/world/europe/country_profiles/3498746.stm

**European Union: CIA World Factbook**
https://www.cia.gov/library/publications/resources/the-world-factbook/geos/ee.html

**The Official Website of the European Union**
europa.eu/index_en.htm

## INDEX

# Picture Credits

All images in this book are in the public domain or have been supplied under license by © Shutterstock.com. The publisher credits the following images as follows:

Page 3: Ms Jane Campbell, page 10: Hadrian, page 11: Ilolab, page 15: Luis Pina Photography, page 17: Smoxx, page 18, 19: Pecold, page 24: Trabantos, page 26, 74: Frederic Legrand-COMEO, page 28: Marco Bicci, page 30: Claudio Divizia, page 31: Drop of Light, page 32: Belish, page 33: Bangkruayan, page 37, 38: Pawel Szczepanski, page 41: Roman Yanushevsky, page 42: Peter Fuchs, page 60: Joerge Steber, page 65: Dennis van der Water, page 70: Forance, page 75: Janossy Gergely, page 76: Photofilippo66, page 78: Christian Mueller, page 80: www.hollandfoto.net, page 86: Photocosmos1.

*To the best knowledge of the publisher, all images not specifically credited are in the public domain. If any image has been inadvertently uncredited, please notify the publisher, so that credit can be given in future printings.*

# Video Credits

Page 21 CGP Grey: http://x-qr.net/1DAF
page 45 European Commission: http://x-qr.net/1DVh
page 65 YortYakr: http://x-qr.net/1Cpr
page 75 National Geographic: http://x-qr.net/1Hf4

# Author

Dominic J. Ainsley is a freelance writer on history, geography, and the arts and the author of many books on travel. His passion for traveling dates from when he visited Europe at the age of ten with his parents. Today, Dominic travels the world for work and pleasure, documenting his experiences and encounters as he goes. He lives in the south of England in the United Kingdom with his wife and two children.